IVY & JOAN

BY JAMES HOGAN

SAMUEL FRENCH

ACKNOWLEDGMENTS

*Sincere thanks to Samuel French for this second edition;
James Illman for typesetting and design; Emma Anacootee-Parmar,
Anthony Biggs, Lynne Miller, Nobby Clark (front cover photograph),
Charles Glanville, Jack Klaff, Amanda Smith,
Nicki Stoddart (United Agents).*

Ivy & Joan was first performed in an earlier version at The Print Room, London, on 14 January 2013 with the following cast:

IVY Lynne Miller
VICTOR Steven Beard

JOAN Lynne Miller
ERIC Steven Beard

Director, Simon Usher
Designer, Carmen Mueck
Lighting Designer, Simon Bennison
Sound Designer, Paul Bull

Production Manager, Andy Beardmore
Stage Manager, Justine Boulton

Ivy & Joan was first performed in this version at The Jermyn Street Theatre on 6 January 2015 with the following cast:

IVY Lynne Miller
VICTOR Jack Klaff

JOAN Lynne Miller
ERIC Jack Klaff

Director, Anthony Biggs
Designer, Victoria Johnstone
Lighting Designer, Charlie Lucas
Sound Designer, Gareth Mcleod
Line producer, Mark Sands

IVY

CHARACTERS

IVY

*60s. A live-in barmaid in charge of the hotel's cocktail bar
who has just been retired.*

VICTOR

a wine waiter, late 50s.

Scene: The staff room of a comfortable hotel
on the Lancashire coast.

Year: 1980

Time: Lunchtime in July. A wedding reception is in progress.

IVY *sits at the table drinking tea from a china cup but no saucer.*

Piano music heard in another part of the hotel.

VICTOR, *the wine waiter, enters carrying a copy of the Racing News.*

VICTOR: What time's your bus? Amanda's been looking for you. She wants to say goodbye.

IVY: Oh, does she? You know what she can do. Little Miss Button Missing can take a running jump.

VICTOR: (*indifferent*) Right.

He sits at the table and opens the Racing News.

IVY *breaks the silence.*

IVY: You're a man of God. Evil begets evil doesn't it? So who's stolen me saucer? This saucer! Victor, who's took it?

VICTOR *looks up briefly, but he is not interested.*

I left it on the draining board. Everyone knows it's mine. Has someone moved it? Was it you? I've looked everywhere. Was it you?

VICTOR: Nope.

IVY: High and low, it's nowhere. Sheraton bone china. Or was it flighty Little Miss Button Missing? I wouldn't put it past her. She'd do it out of spite. She would too. Sheraton bone china, Tupperware, *she* wouldn't know the difference, would she? Knows nowt about wine neither. Chardonnay's a perfume! Huh! "I think you mean Chanel, love, don't you?"

Ought button up her blouse an'all. Don't you think so? (*beat*) No, why do I bother? All the managers are of the male species.

VICTOR: (*matter of fact*) She's attractive.

IVY: Aren't you on *now*? They've started, haven't they?

VICTOR: (*looks at his watch*) Not yet! They're still eating. There's no one in the bar.

IVY: Little Miss Button Missing's in there on her own.

VICTOR: She'll manage all right.

IVY: If you say so.

> **IVY** *sips tea.*

> *The music stops.*

What a racket. Hark at it. Friend of the happy couple on the piano. Honky tonky plonky? Liberace I don't think. You only get what you pay for, or don't pay for. Cut price wedding, cut price music, cut price bride an'all. I mean it. Yesterday that dress was her bedroom curtains.

VICTOR: *Gone with the Wind.* In *Gone with the Wind* Scarlet O'Hara makes a dress out of the curtains. Vivien Leigh.

IVY: The groom's old enough to be her father. Another chequebook wedding.

VICTOR: Tight bastard actually. Wouldn't breathe out if he didn't have to. Drives his own van. Too stingy to employ anyone. He owns the furniture shop just off the square. Bradshaw's.

IVY: Oh, them, oh dear. Oh well, she'll allus have a table to eat off. His carnation's droopy. That's not a good sign either.

VICTOR: Trust you Ivy.

IVY: He's past it. You can always tell, can't you? Vic, have *you* seen me saucer?

VICTOR: No. I have not seen your saucer. How would I know it was yours?

IVY: The pattern! Sheraton bone china. Little Miss Button Missing knew. "Whose is this?", she said. "Whose is this pretty saucer? Ivy's?" (*beat*) She's binned it. I bet she has an'all. Just like her. "Whose is this pretty saucer?" Bang, straight in the bin. If I was a witch I'd put a curse on her.

VICTOR: Ivy, give over.

IVY: I would! Hubble bubble at the double vanish. You're a cockroach now, love. Crawl away.

VICTOR: Mumbo jumbo? They'll lock you up.

IVY: I'll crown you in a minute. I'm serious. Little Miss Button missing, by God she's got it coming.

VICTOR: Give over, I said. I'm busy.

IVY: If I see her before I go…

VICTOR: Don't spoil the wedding. There's folk out there enjoying the'sel. Crikey, if anyone could hear you now… Give over!

Pause.

Aren't you going somewhere?

IVY: I am. My friend Inky in Manchester, why?

VICTOR: Witches and Hobgoblins? Good job it's not Wales. They still burn witches there. I wish I'd gone for a walk now. But for the rain… It's your own fault all this.

IVY: My *fault*?

VICTOR: You invite antagonism, don't you know?

IVY: I've worked in this hotel forty years.

VICTOR: I know. Don't miss your bus.

Pause. She stares at him. She's hurt.

IVY: You can put the flags out when I'm gone. I'm legally entitled to remain on these premises until midnight tonight. Midnight tonight.

She sips her tea.

I know too much. That's why they want me out.

VICTOR: No. You only think you do.

IVY: I do know! So what do *you* know stuck in your Racing News? I twigged it straight away. The place is crawling with executives from head office. Open your eyes, Vic, and switch on your other brain cell. They were in my bar having a right pow-wow. They all end up in my bar, don't they? Sat at the other end, confidential conversations? Huh. They don't know I can lip read.

VICTOR: (*makes a note on his paper*) Blue-eyed Boy. Three twenty at York. Ten to one. That's a winner.

IVY: I'm only the first, the first to go. (*beat*) Mr. Timmins might call *you* into the office. All depending on what Little Miss Button Missing thinks of *you*.

VICTOR: Your tea's going cold.

IVY: No matter, as long it's hot to start with. (*pause*)

When I walk out of here... This is the last half hour of my forty years in charge of the cocktail bar. We never think of that, do we, the last half hour; the last half hour of things.

VICTOR: Oh but I do. The last half hour of my marriage. Me and Muriel, I remember our last breakfast together. For the first time in twelve years she refused to slice the top off my boiled eggs. So I grabbed my coat, walked out. Never went back.

IVY: Slice the top off your boiled eggs?

VICTOR: Well, my mother always did, and tied my shoe laces.

IVY: When did you leave home?

VICTOR: I got married when I was thirty seven.

IVY: Twelve years married, you didn't slice the top off your own boiled eggs fall that time?

VICTOR: It was a thing between us. But all good things come to an end. You're not missing much leaving now. You're not missing anything. I remember when the cocktail bar was full of celebrities. All the stars of the summer shows. An autograph hunter's paradise. Comedians, entertainers, actors.

IVY: You don't have to tell *me!* I've seen 'em all I have. Les Dawson, Russ Conway, Alma Cogan, the girl with a giggle in her voice. She died of cancer, thirty four years old. Mind you, I go back to Dickie Henderson. What a lovely man an'all. And *he* died of cancer. Terry-Thomas. Remember Terry-Thomas? All those funny films. *Private's Progress*: (*as Terry-Thomas*) "You're an absolute sha'r!" The perfect English gentleman he was. (*beat*) He was! And *he* got Parkinsons. Why do these terrible things happen to such nice people?

VICTOR: Oh, well *you* needn't worry. (*reflects*) As we get older these things happen.

IVY: I know. In one day my life turns upside down.

VICTOR: Only if you think about it. (*smug*) I've learned to live in the moment. I've had to. Tomorrow comes tomorrow and not before.

IVY: So I see. The horses, losing your wages. Here today, gone today, penniless by tea-time. A live-in job and staff meals, you always know where your next meal's coming from. But that's *false* security.

VICTOR: What time's your bloody bus?

Pause.

IVY: Can I say something?

VICTOR: You've done nowt else since you walked in.

IVY: Add up all what you've lost. All these years your wages go straight into the betting shop. Everywhere else it's economical misery. There's no visitors now. They all go to Benidorm. The pier's only open weekends. If it wasn't for wedding parties this hotel would…. (*beat*) But the betting shop stays open for layabouts. I can't work it out. You an'all throwing your money away.

VICTOR: It's an investment. One day I'll win a big one, an accumulator.

IVY: A what?

VICTOR: An accumulator. If you don't know racing, you won't know what it is.

IVY: (*taps her handbag*) This is my accumulator, my savings book. I'm an outsider. At least *you're* still talkin' to me. About the only one who is. Thank you for that.

VICTOR: (*bored with her*) Eh? What's up now?

VICTOR *makes another note.* **IVY** *looks on.*

IVY: D'you know how long I've had it, this cup and saucer? Forty years. On my last day the saucer goes missing. In pieces, I dare say, but no-one owns up.

VICTOR: Buy another one.

IVY: If it's broken, I want to know.

VICTOR: I see. You want closure.

IVY: Sheraton bone china. My friend Inky gave it me. Inky coz she writes nice letters. Copper-plate handwriting with a fountain pen. She still does do, write nice letters. Ever since the war. My friend Inky from the WAAFs. Don't laugh, me and Inky in the Women's Auxiliary Air Force. More like Fred Karno's Army. Left right, left right, or right left right left, *we* didn't know. (*beat*) Did you do National Service? Vic. (*beat*) No, you didn't, I can tell. Were you a conchy?

VICTOR: You what? A conchy!

IVY: Conscientious objector.

He lowers his racing paper, shaking his head in disgust.

You never talk about it. Gen'ly men who keep quiet about the war…

VICTOR: D'you mind! Catering corp. I were never a conchy!

IVY: (*unimpresssed*) Catering Corp, oh.

VICTOR: What d'you mean "Oh"? I just told you. I were never a conchy!

Pause. He stares at her waiting for an answer.

They all say that "oh". "The catering Corp, oh". But you can't fight a war an empty stomach. I did my bit me; and my father before me. In the first World War my father served in the 8th East Lancashire Regiment and fought in the trenches. So bugger off.

He buries himself in his racing paper and turns his back on her.

IVY: I'm only talkin', Vic.

VICTOR: Celebrating your forty-year dash for freedom? And now you want a public enquiry to find your broken saucer.

IVY: Broken. I thought so. (*pause*) I hope the bus is on time. Inky said she'll meet me. Manchester Victoria. D'you know Manchester?

VICTOR: No.

She sips her tea.

IVY: (*subdued, thoughtful*) Sheraton bone china. I want to show Inky I've still got it. Listen, if you find it… Eh, the dustbins! (*she stands up*)

VICTOR: Don't be so daft. Ivy, you can't go rooting through dustbins now, you'll miss your bus.

IVY: Vic, if it's broken, if you find the pieces, keep them for me. Will you keep them for me? I'm due back in two weeks. I've an appointment at the Town Hall. Housing Department. I'm hoping for a council flat, two bedrooms. You see, when Harry gets back.

VICTOR: Harry. Here we go.

IVY: I put my name down years ago. I qualify now. Mind you, this was a bolt out the blue. Two week's notice. I said to Timmins "give over, I'm goin' now". We've no rights, have we, live-in staff. (*pause*) Vic, where will you go when...

VICTOR *cocks his ear.*

Go to the town Hall. Put your name down. How old are you now? Fifty seven, fifty eight? Sixty soon then. (*beat*) The thing is, Harry won't know where I've gone. When he comes to find me...

VICTOR *lowers his paper. This mention of* **HARRY** *is weird.*

We'll get married straight away of course. Oh, he's such a rascal, my Harry. "Ivy, what I don't do to you on our wedding night won't be worth doin'." A right rascal, but I like a man who thinks highly of himself. He could turn up tomorrow, any day. D'you know what he looks like? Did I show you his photo.

VICTOR: (*stopping her with a gesture*) Ivy...

IVY *rummages through her handbag.*

IVY: It's all agreed. We'll get married at the Town Hall. The reception won't be here. Not in this dump. I know what lurks in the kitchens. Enough wildlife to film a nature programme.

IVY *shows the photo to* **VICTOR**.

That's my Harry. They don't make'em like that any more.

VICTOR: (*stares at the photo*) I wonder what he looks like now.

IVY: Head waiter. Savoy trained.

VICTOR: Good looking man I will say. (*returning the photo*)
   Windy day. Where was it taken?

IVY: The Lakes on our day off. Windermere. (*putting the photo
   in her handbag*) The best head waiter this hotel ever had.
   They took him for granted, of course, like everyone else.
   Live-in staff were never off duty. Now it's all legalized, eh?
   Little Miss Button Missing doesn't know how lucky she is.

VICTOR: Ivy, I can't concentrate.

   Pause.

IVY: Eh you, never mind them horses! You heed my warning.

VICTOR: The witch's warning?

IVY: No, Vic. Plain old common sense!

VICTOR: Sorry, Ivy. I place my faith in God.

IVY: God, he says, huh! The betting shop. Is that allowed?

VICTOR: I'm not a Catholic!

IVY: Listen, I know things God doesn't tell you. I'm warning
   you, Vic.

VICTOR: I know! The witch's warning! I'm quaking in my
   boots!

IVY: Stop acting the goat. I'm talkin'. When they sat in my bar, them executives... You wait and see, more redundancies. If they want a strike, they're going the right way about it.

VICTOR: You *don't* know.

IVY: I *do* know. Don't fall on the sword of ignorance. Listen to me. You'll thank me one day. Oh, you listen to the Bible, I know you do. Begat begat begat and all that. I believed in the Bible once, every word of it, but not any more.

VICTOR: What changed your mind?

IVY: I read it.

VICTOR: (*looks at his watch*) If you want to start a strike, you've twenty minutes to go before the Exodus. Why not catch the bus, love? Go in peace, and I wish you all the very best in the future. (*false smile*)

She is silenced for a moment. Sips her tea, and then decides to speak seriously.

IVY: Them executives and Little Miss Button Missing were drinking till the small hours. "You're working late, Ivy!" I take pride in my bar, I said. Every glass is polished before I go to bed. I turned the music off so I could listen. Hush hush, but I can lip read. (*beat*) So I'm a witch, am I? I bet if I read your tea-leaves...

VICTOR *Shrugs it off.*

Don't scoff. I have a moral duty to tell people what my psychic gift tells me. Let me see your cup.

VICTOR: It's a tea-bag.

IVY: Tea stains'll do. Let me look.

VICTOR: (*beat, he wants to put her off*) Executives you say. What executives?

IVY: The penny's dropped, has it? Them executives! Your cup, Victor please. Give it me.

VICTOR: No!

IVY: Come on, why not?

VICTOR: It's a Pagan thing, isn't it?

IVY: Them executives. Why d'you think they're staying the night? An inspection? Oh, no. That's not the real reason. And what's your destiny? I do need your tea-cup please.

VICTOR: No!

He puts his paper down and rises from the table.

Goodbye, Ivy. Have a nice journey to Manchester.

IVY: What're you doin' here? The reception's starting.

VICTOR: Mr. Timmins said it's all right.

IVY: What's alright? Wait till he calls *you* into the office.

VICTOR *makes to go.*

Vic! Them executives, your name was mentioned.

VICTOR *waits*.

They spent a lot of time in the staff quarters, didn't they?
Then ended up in my bar. Mr Timmins bowing and
scraping.

VICTOR: No one mentioned my name. You're making it up.

IVY: One of them's got a tape measure. Like a builder's tape
measure. He put it on the table. Now if that's not clue…

VICTOR: When? My day off? They're refurbishing. Mr
Timmins told everyone they're refurbishing.

IVY: Ties undone, flirting with Little Miss Button Missing. I
would never presume to socialize with area management.
Krug champagne. Krug! She didn't pay for it. (*assuredly*)
She'll pay for it on her back.

VICTOR: Refurbishing now turns into a fiendish management
plot. You're still at it, Ivy, to the bitter end, making
mischief.

IVY: Vic, if you stick your head in the sand any longer, your
backside'll get sunburn!

He makes to go again.

All right, refurbishing, but what for? Harry once said: "To
work in this hotel you need eyes in the back of your head
and a knife-proof vest". He was right. (*beat*) Go on if you
want too! You're on duty.

VICTOR: (*hesitates*) What about *your* fatal destiny? This Harry
fellah. D'you even know where he is? Is that all you've got

to go on, that old photo? Dream on. You're bloody daft, you are.

Silence. **VICTOR** *sits down, he pushes his tea-mug across the table.*

Go on. Them executives. You tell me what the Devils are up to.

She takes the tea-mug, but doesn't look into it yet.

IVY: What it is is this. They want to convert the staff wing into eight new single rooms and a nursery. Little Miss Button Missing is on their side. Spying on the rest of us, anyone who doesn't fit in. Like me, my face doesn't fit, does it? And my room's a double. Which we need when Harry…

VICTOR: You said my name was mentioned. Little Miss Button Missing. I know what she's like. Butter wouldn't melt in her mouth.

IVY: It wouldn't melt if it went right through her and came out the other end. They've installed her in my bar, expecting me to work my notice under her authority.

VICTOR: What did she say about me?

He sits down.

IVY: I only heard your name.

VICTOR: My name. Anything else? Yes? No? (*sniggers*) I thought so. You heard nowt! Don't miss your bus.

IVY: After breakfast. I nipped down for my specs. I was wearing my slippers… The pink bunny rabbits Inky gave me. Nice and warm. Lo and behold, there she is re-arranging my bar. Little Miss Button Missing. I said "What you doin'ere? We don't open till lunchtime". So she goes "Ivy, what have you got on your feet, pink bunny rabbits?" Out loud like, to show me up. Top button of her blouse undone as usual; that early in the morning, disgusting. And purple beads, hardly the thing with freckles. Her teeth don't suit her face. Where did they find her? (*beat*) Or did Mr Timmins find her? He goes kerb crawling, you know. I've seen'im, five miles an hour. Night blindness he calls it. Huh.

She peers down into his tea-mug.

VICTOR: Anything else? (*To himself*) I just might catch the four twenty at York. Nip out for five minutes.

IVY: Re-arrange my bar! Ow dare she! "Listen you", I said. "I'll wipe that smirk of your bloody face."

VICTOR: With a knife in your hand. Is that true?

IVY: That's a lie. I were slicing a lemon, that's all. My hot water and lemon. Then she started. "Look sharp, Ivy. What y'doin' standin' there for?" Cheeky monkey. "What y'doin' standin' there for? What are you doing with that knife, oh Ivy!" So I thought "Right, I know what to do. See Mr Timmins." Defend myself before she ruins my reputation.

VICTOR: That says it all. You did *yourself* in. How stupid can you get? You make a formal complaint to the Manager about another member of staff. Nobody does that. In the process you tell him you had a row with a knife in your hand.

IVY: I'm not afraid of managers, Vic.

VICTOR: A dishonourable discharge. Serves you right.

IVY: What did you say? (*pause*) I went straight to his office, didn't knock neither, and I told him: "A teenage tart, a slut tells her seniors what to do! Just eighteen in charge of a cocktail bar, *my* cocktail bar. Have you seen what she does?", I said. "Cork in the wine every time. A Bloody Mary's vodka, tomato juice and HP sauce!" She can't read the labels, that's why, and she needs a calculator to multiply by ten.

VICTOR: She's only just started.

IVY: "Oh dear me!", he says, "Ivy, the things you say, I'm stunned". Stunned I don't think. They couldn't stun him in the electric chair. Then he goes on. An adverse report apparently. Rude to customers as well? I've never been rude to a customer. Perfect good conduct me. "Oh, a warning?" I said. "You know what to can do with your warning. Stick it up yer jumper." That was it. Two weeks notice. Two weeks in disgrace as far as I'm concerned. "So forget it. I'm going now!" (*beat*) I've written to Harry.

VICTOR *puts his racing paper down. He shuffles uncomfortably.*

VICTOR: Harry. So you do know where he is.

IVY: Care of the Merchant Navy Association. (*confident*) They'll forward it. They'll forward my letter.

Pause.

I rang up Inky. I said "Inky, you wouldn't believe it! This eighteen years old skips in, born with ear-phones on and I'm a goner…"

VICTOR: Sounds like Mr Timmins seized his chance.

IVY: (*looking into his tea-mug*) Aye! To get my room off of me. They'll have yours next.

VICTOR: You walked into the trap, Ivy. Anyway, you've got somewhere to go. Think yourself lucky. Your friend whatsername.

IVY: Inky. Crikey, where's me bus ticket?

Rummages in her handbag.

VICTOR: The Merchant Navy Association, will they really know where Harry is? How do you know he's on a British ship? You might as well tie your letter to a balloon. When did you last hear from him? He could be dead.

IVY: (*grumbling*) Rude to residents. I were never ever rude to a resident. That stupid vegetarian had a fit that's all.

(*posh*) "Is this salad suitable for vegetarians?"

So I say: "It's a salad, madam."

(*posh*) "Yes, I know, but what's in it? Is it *entirely* suitable for vegetarians?"

"I assume so, madam. I'm sure a caterpillar would enjoy it."

Unfortunately, there *was* a caterpillar in it.

VIC: I agree with you there. We should eat meat. Live animals is God's way of keeping food fresh.

IVY: Normally you can't see a green caterpillar in watercress, but this one was crawling along the plate.

VICTOR: It's in the Bible, the fish in the sea and the fowls in the air.

He buries himself in the Racing News.

IVY: I'm glad I'm going. You should know those horses by heart, all the names. You've been staring at them long enough. Vic, give me some names. I'll see what I get. Go on, what are the names?

VICTOR: If you're psychic, you tell *me*.

IVY: I *am* psychic. Remember when I saw your Grandmother's ghost?

VICTOR: So you say. She was wearing her pink cardigan, Eh? Eternal life for the soul is one thing, but not even Marks & Sparks say their cardigans last *that* long.

IVY: Hold on. I might get a flash. (*gazes down into his cup*) Say the names.

VICTOR: (*hesitant*) Fleur de Lys.

IVY: What?

VICTOR: Fleur de Lys. That's the name. French.

IVY: French.

VICTOR: Maybe you need a French cup. Fleur de Lys, Dusty's Double, Hell's Angel.

IVY closes her eyes to see what she gets.

IVY: Say again.

VICTOR: Fleur de Lys, Dusty's Double, Hell's Angel. What are you doing?

IVY: I'll ask my spirit guides, Zaxmar and Spock.

VICTOR: Zaxmar and who?

IVY: Spock.

VICTOR: Spock is in *Star Trek*.

IVY: There's more than one Spock in the universe. Dusty's Double! That's the winner.

VICTOR: Dusty's Double, eh? That's funny. That race was an hour ago. Got nowhere. Might as well have had a wooden leg. If you ask me, Zaxmar and Spock are a bit behind the times. Listen, Ivy. You can't be a spiritualist in your place of work. And one other thing, your washing: in staff quarters we are not condisposed to your knickers on the line.

IVY: So it's all of you. I see now what's been going on.

VICTOR: You can't blame us. We've done nothing. Mind you, you wouldn't win a popularity contest round'ere.

IVY: And who d'you think *you're* talking to! Are *you* the ring leader?

VICTOR: I rest my case. You've gone sour, Ivy. Sour face, sour... And we all know why, waiting for Harry. Oh, never mind. *(beat, offhand)* They're upgrading the hotel. Needs money spent on it. But you've talked yourself out of a job and into your friend Inky's spare room. End of story. Don't blame me. *(beat)* If you must know I volunteered to sit here and see you off the premises. I volunteered, so I don't *have* to. Mr Timmins wants to make sure you... Don't make a fuss infront the guests.

IVY: Oh, does he.

VICTOR: Where's your luggage? There's nothing worse than someone leaving who doesn't actually go.

IVY: Well, thank you. Thank you very much!

Silence.

All in a single day. I'm upside down now. Oh, I do know whether I'm coming or going. I'm going. The cornerstone of this hotel. If people knew... They all know my bar. They all know Ivy, all over town. No, the whole County! *(beat)* My regulars, they'll be wondering where I've gone. *(beat)* Tell them Harry came to collect me. He will do when he gets my letter. Maybe we'll get married in Manchester.

I wonder if he's got it already? (*She seems suddenly full of hope*)

VICTOR *is moved and looks at her.*

VICTOR: (*humouring her*) Manchester? Not the Town Hall? Will I be invited? Sixty miles to Manchester, but for you, Ivy....

IVY: (*abruptly cutting in*) Little Miss Button Missing this morning... "Ivy, if you've nothing to do, vacuum the carpet in the hall. They want it spic and span for the wedding". Cooeee! Iveee! Jib jib jib jib jib!

"You know what you can do", I said. "Listen, I vacuum my bar, my bar only. As far as that door and no further. You have no authority over me".

VICTOR: (*about to stand up*) Let's get your luggage. Is it at the staff entrance? I'll take you to the bus stop.

IVY: Wait a minute. The lad on the door's helping me, so there! I'm not staff now. So I will leave by the *main* door. I want to sneak round to see the wedding cake. Let's see if Little Miss Button Missing can cope in the bar on her own. Have you seen it, the wedding cake? I normally snaffle a piece for my tea, on the QT like, but not this time. I won't be here when they cut it.

VICTOR: (*sighs, looks at his racing paper*) There's a winner. Cheeky Chappie! (*writes it down*)

IVY: Horses. I can't see the fascination. (*beat*) So who did break my saucer? Sheraton bone china.

VICTOR: I'm sorry about your saucer.

IVY: No you're not. Now listen. One more thing, Victor. If Mr. Timmins summons you to the office, be ready for him. Mention the magic word compensation you won't go far wrong. (*warmer*) You and your 'orses. Never mind your'orses. You can't buy luck, you know. Luck just comes your way. Out of the blue I received a letter from Inky. This one.

She takes a letter out of her handbag and reads:

Listen. "My dear Ivy…"

VICTOR: Don't miss your bus.

IVY: (*fadingly*) …"It's not been the same since my beloved husband passed away. Di da di daaa… Can you take your holidays early? I could do with the company." They'd no children, which normally means a house full of dogs. So there's only a budgie to feed.

I phoned her after they got married. I said "what's it like being married?"

"Oh Lord", she said, "I'm never out of bed!" Up and down like a bride's nightie.

She puts the letter back in her handbag.

She writes every Christmas. But last Christmas when the letter came, a shiver went up my spine before I even opened it. I knew it was bad news.

"Dear Ivy …

VICTOR: (*standing*) If you're all right then, I *might* catch the three twenty.

VICTOR *stuffs his pen in his pocket.*

IVY: Don't you want to see me off? Do your bloody'orses then! Another tenner gone. You're a fool to yourself, Vic. Money's the next best thing to blood. You can't do without it! You won't listen, will you?

She looks into his tea-mug.

VICTOR: (*dismissive*) Look, don't worry about me. I'm retiring soon to my mother's bungalow. She's eighty next year. She needs lookin' after.

IVY: *You* need lookin' after. Will she slice the top off your boiled eggs?

VICTOR: (*smug*) She's a nice two bedroomed bungalow which I will inherit.

IVY: I hope she leaves you the egg-cups as well. (*she looks down into his tea-cup*) Just as I thought! Storm clouds gathering. Two men. Two men in an argument. One in a position of authority, and who do we think that might be? You might be getting them boiled eggs sooner than you think.

VICTOR: If you spent less time on that rubbish and more time in the here and now...

IVY: Here and now? Upstairs watching tele? Nowt in your pocket till next pay day. Living off the chef's greasy hot-pot. He puts left-overs in it. And chicken feet in the stock.

I said: "They might like that in Shanghai, but don't give it to me". *You're* too busy with the horses.

VICTOR *has second thoughts, waits and sits down.*

IVY *looks into his tea-mug.*

Changed your mind, have you?

VICTOR: No! I said I'd see you off the premises. Your friend Inky won't want all this. Jesus, when you fetch up in Manchester.

IVY *puts the tea-mug down with a bang.*

IVY: You think I'm barmy, don't you? You all do! Am I barmy because I dream of love? You threw love away. You walked out on your wife when she forgot to slice the top off your boiled eggs! Oh, what a calamity!

VICTOR: (*bored*) She didn't forget! It was unconsciously deliberate. I read the signs in humans, not tea-cups.Mind your own business anyway.

VICTOR *starts to rise from the table.*

IVY: Wait! I want you to read this! Harry's letter.

She takes a battered old envelope out of her handbag.

You read it. Go on, read it. Go on.

VICTOR *looks at the stamp.*

VICTOR: Hong Kong aye. (*hands it back*)

IVY: No, read it. Look, it's filled with writing edge to edge. That means he wanted to say more.

VICTOR: Or ran out of paper.

She knows the letter by heart and reads it from memory.

IVY: "Dear Ivy,

As you see, I write from a far off place. I have spent many months on cruise ships around the world. The money is good, and the places we go ashore are fascinating. But I still read a lot. Forgive me for absenting myself without saying goodbye. I know that was hurtful, and I'm sorry if I have let you down. I was not ready to go steady. And I always planned to travel and see the world. A bird on the wing, never to settle on any branch for long. I do think of the crazy hotel sometimes and our short time together. Perhaps too good to last. Some things are not to be. How does it Go? "It would take Oberon and all his magic dust to remedy all the unhappinesses there are."... Perhaps when I return, even if your life has turned another page, and a better one, which I am sure it will. I hope we can still say hello..."

She weeps silently.

VICTOR *puts his paper aside and gets up as if to comfort her. But it is a feeble attempt.*

VICTOR: Quite a poet, your Harry. You said he was a rascal. D'you want another cup? This is cold. Ivy.

IVY: Like I said, as long as it's hot to start with.

IVY *composes herself.*

IVY: He won't know where to find me. If I give you Inky's address… Her phone number… Mr Timmins says the office'll forward my post, but I don't trust them. They're glad to see the back of me. So are you. What did you just say? "There's nothing worse than someone leaving who…"

VICTOR: I were joking.

IVY: …who never actually goes. But before I go, I've something else to show you. Sit down.

VICTOR *sits down.*

IVY *takes her savings book out of her handbag. She hands it to* **VICTOR**.

My savings.

VICTOR: Your savings book?

IVY: Have a look. The money I've saved up. Go on, it's important. Vic, it's never too late to start saving. Money in the bank. The trouble is you can't look after yourself. I've seen what you eat. Chef's leftovers and chip butties.

VICTOR: I like chip butties.

IVY: The nearest you ever get to eating vegetables is mint sauce.

VICTOR *opens the savings book. He is taken aback.*

VICTOR: Bloody Norah. Can *I* marry you?

IVY: See? You'll never win that much on one your whatsits, accumulators. My wages go into that savings book every week since I started work. Now then. Forty years ago. A chamber maid until I was eighteen and then they gave me the cocktail bar.

VICTOR: So you were the Little Miss Button Missing then.

IVY: I was.

Piano music is heard again.

He's off again. You'd better go.

VICTOR: Don't worry about me.

IVY: Did you know? This hotel was owned by the Pemberton family. Before your time. Well, Mr Pemberton wanted his key staff to live in. On the spot see. Never late for work. No fool was he! There was me, Harry and a few others. We all lived up top. I remember two Irish waitresses shared a room. I had my own room. Harry had the room next to mine. *(beat)* Yes, I know what you're thinking and you're right. Youthful joy got in the way of common sense. There'd been a wedding that day and... Well, some champagne left over. Harry and me, we didn't stint ourselves. I told you, he *was* a rascal. He was *that* night.

The music stops.

He slept like a baby with his arms all round me, and I stayed awake all night to savour it, his warm body. *(pause)* But I fell asleep in the end and he slipped away.

VICTOR *places the savings book on the table.*

VICTOR: That's a lot of money, Ivy.

IVY: If you hadn't spent all your money on the'orses…
Where's your self-respect?

*VICTOR rises from his seat in a manner to suggest it's time she
went for her bus.*

D'you need that paper? Give me the front bit.

*She takes it and wraps up her tea-cup. The tea-cup is slipped
into her pocket.*

IVY: I bought a new outfit yesterday. Well, when Harry gets
back… R J Taylor's in the Square. I've always wanted to
shop there. R J Taylor's. That's where that vegetarian cow
goes for her dresses, (*posh*) Gowns, so sorry.

VICTOR: Give over. If I'd sunk my teeth into a caterpillar…

IVY: I can afford a chauffeur to Manchester, but I'm not
touching any of that money.

VICTOR: Take the bus for now. I'll carry your things to the bus
stop.

IVY: Inky's meeting me anyway. She's doing toad in the hole.
Toad in the hole for sentimental reasons. Like in the
WAAFS. One sausage each then, but tonight we're having
two.

She sees that VICTOR has gone. She is about to follow.

Piano music.

Vic, you haven't got my address. Vic! Don't make me late!

She grabs VICTOR'*s pencil and scribbles the address on a scrap of paper.*

Honest to God, I'll be late for my own funeral.

Oh! *(Picks up the savings book)* Harry love, the money! Not only our bread and butter, our passport to dignity, you and me. What would we do without this? I keep tellin' you. Hark at my wisdom, love. It won't do you no harm. You've been gone too long an' all. Wait when I see you, I won't half give you what for. This money's for you. I told you in a letter care of the Merchant Seaman's Association. I'll have to write again now. *(Beat)* Vic, don't let the bus go without me!

Exit. She goes to Manchester.

THE END

JOAN

CHARACTERS

JOAN
mid 50s.

ERIC
her husband, also 50s.

Scene: Their kitchen

Year: The present during October.

Time: Late-afternoon.

*Music: October (from Tchaikovsky's The Seasons) played on the
piano.*

JOAN *sits at the table on which there are the remains of a light meal
for two, an unopened bottle of Chianti Classico and two unused
glasses. There is a suitcase on the floor near the door.*

*Note: The pauses marked in the text are mostly short breaks when the
character has not decided what to say.*

JOAN: Why did you say that? I'm a deeply foolish woman.

ERIC: (*indifferent*) Did I?

JOAN: Yesterday.

ERIC: Yesterday?!

JOAN: (*beat*) I object to the word "deeply". We can all be a
bit stupid, but "deeply" is so unforgiving. There *is* such a
thing as forgiveness. You should know.

   ERIC *sighs.*

   Make an effort, Eric. It's not as if I... At least open the
wine. There's still time. If we don't drink all of it, so what?

ERIC: You open it if you want to.

JOAN: Nice wine from Portoguaro.

ERIC: GRUaro. PortoGRUaro.

JOAN: You carried it all the way from Italy. Now you don't
want it.

ERIC: It's only Chianti Classico. We could have got it at the end of the street.

JOAN: The best wine is always the wine in front of you. PortoGRUaro. Where exactly is it? Where is it in relation to Venice? Five miles, ten miles?

ERIC: Kilometres. Joan, we're not on holiday any more.

JOAN: Can't we talk about it? (*beat*) I can still see it all in my mind's eye. Where are your pictures? On your computer?

ERIC: Digital technology. We should be grateful.

JOAN: Here begineth and endeth the first lesson, His Holiness Pope Sanctimonio the first of Croydon has spoken.

ERIC: (*quiet*) Joan, shut up.

JOAN: You shut up about technology and progress. Huh. The inventors of the mobile phone have forced the entire population of the world to type with one finger. Now is that progress? I'd much rather share our memories of Venice. The place itself, not what you think of me. (*beat*) Venice. Come on, what's your lasting impression of Venice?

Pause.

Never mind. I've blotted my copybook again.

ERIC *leaves the table abruptly and goes to stand by the window.* JOAN *looks at him for a moment and then picks up her pen.*

It was a lovely holiday. Thank you. Churches, paintings, music. Especially the golden thing in St. Mark's cathedral.

ERIC: Thing. If you mean the Pala d'Oro in the Basilica di San Marco...

JOAN: Yes.

ERIC: ...the finest expression of Byzantine art...

JOAN: Pala what?

ERIC: Pala d'Oro it contains the relics of St. Mark, the Evangelist... The whole building is known as the Chiesa d'Oro, the Church of Gold. Didn't you read the guide? I think we're sharing *my* memories, rather than yours.

JOAN: Solid gold, is it? (*pause*) Is it solid gold?

ERIC: I don't know.

JOAN: Didn't *you* read the guide? A gold altarpiece. I wonder what it's worth? Enough to house all the homeless in Europe.

ERIC: (*sniggers*) Here we go.

JOAN: Eric, if the world really cared about the poor, there wouldn't be any poor. When I say that I mean it. (*beat*) Snigger on. You always do. I don't know why you're so... (*waves the notepad*) Is it this? Is it this now, my writing? (*beat*) I know my limitations, Eric. I'm not trying to be a travel writer. It's not a book anyway. (*beat*) I wish I could write. Not nearly as messy as painting. Writing is... it... It's how we share experience and values, rather better than Venetian gold artefacts, which just sit there looking expensive.

ERIC: Attracting millions of tourists, who spend money. The Pala d'Oro also shares its value. You were too busy chasing your poet friend to notice the art and the architecture of the City of Dreams. Sorry, Joan, but we've had this conversation before. Did you pack your paints?

JOAN: I took it all in. Cathedrals, palaces, paintings…

ERIC: Basilicas. (*pause*) My lasting impression? All right; how strong they were in their faith in the fifteenth century. So many churches, great and small.

JOAN: You lit a candle in every one of them. That's why I went for my walks.

ERIC: And you turned to look at every man in a white suit, in case it was the dashing poet.

JOAN: Signor Dottore Marcello di Eduardo…

ERIC: You believe that's his real name? Huh.

JOAN: He's not a poet. He writes poetry now and then. But he remembers the history of Venice by heart in every detail. Art and music, and how the Venetians skinned their enemies alive in St. Mark's Square.

ERIC: Piazza San Marco.

JOAN: Skinned alive. Stick to the point, Eric; not the bloody street names. Skinned alive, have you any idea of the suffering? Your fellow men calmly slicing off your skin from head to toe? Blood-soaked, still alive, left hanging there for all to see. The victim's eyes ask "Why? Oh, why? Oh, why?" The artistic Venetian authorities also tortured their victims in the dungeon, walls so thick no one hears the screams. No forgiveness there either. Inside the prison they're breaking someone's bones. Outside they're calmly tucking into cannelloni and Chianti.

ERIC: (*sarcastic*) Chianti Classico?

JOAN: That's what I think of Venice. I'll write what I feel.

ERIC: Well, you've got your Chianti. That's a start.

JOAN: (*writing it down) Blood… and… gold*. The title of my poem is *Blood and Gold*.

ERIC: (*offhand*) Whatever happened to the novel?

JOAN: I'm writing a poem. A poem, why not?

Pause.

ERIC: Where are your paints?

JOAN: (*beat, evading the question*) *Blood and Gold*. Gold and Blood? No, doesn't scan. Mind you, there's a good deal of mould in Venice as well as gold. Mould, gold? We either see what we want to see; or what's actually there. Crumbling sepulchres of mould and ancient gold. That's how he put it, Signor Dottore…

ERIC: Yes, we know all about him. Thank you!

JOAN: We see what we want to see, believe what we want to
    believe.

ERIC: (*beat*) Who was he really?

JOAN *shuffles uncomfortably.*

JOAN: I told you. Signor Dottore Marcello di Eduardo. He sat
    at my table in the square… (*deliberately correct*) Piazza San
    Marco. A fine gentleman. Calm, softly spoken… He made
    me feel like whatsername in the film. Before we left, that
    film…

ERIC: *The Wings of the Dove.*

JOAN: Helena Bonham Carter. He said I looked like Helena
    Bonham Carter.

ERIC: You look nothing like Helena Bonham Carter.

JOAN: He even called me Helena.

ERIC: You look nothing like Helena Bonham Carter! Joan,
    he says the same thing to every woman he meets there.
    Flattery. Oh how romantic, huh.

JOAN: All perfectly innocent. You know it was.

ERIC: Adultery begins in the mind, not in bed.

Pause.

Approached by a strange man, you should have walked
away. (*beat*) No surprises, you're writing another love story.

JOAN: A poem!

ERIC: By the way, the feedback from the leader of your
    writing circle: I'm not sure comparison with Barbara
    Cartland is a compliment. (*beat*) Stick to painting.

Pause.

JOAN: Signor Dottore Marcello…

ERIC: Di Eduardo.

JOAN: …is my mentor now When I finish it, he said, send it
    to him, my impressions of Venice. Writing makes a change
    from painting a bowl of fruit. You always eat it.

ERIC: Why waste good fruit? Paint our church. It doesn't go
    off in a week.

JOAN: I know. It takes centuries. I'm not inspired by brick
    walls and plain windows, and it doubles up as a crêche.
    The vicar plays a guitar.

ERIC: Rather well.

JOAN: Christmas at St. Lukes. Our trendy vicar sits on a
    plastic chair to play *Silent Night* on his guitar, shortly to be
    joined by his twelve year old daughter on the recorder to
    jolly up *Good King Wenceslas*. I can't wait.

    ERIC *shows impatience, banging the window-sill.*

    Shush. I'm trying to remember what we did in Venice!

ERIC: Oh. So we're not sharing *our* memories of the holiday.

JOAN: You can read it when I've finished.

> **ERIC** *moves closer to her.*

ERIC: (*softer*) Joan, you're here now. Here! Here they want
you to paint, not write. D'you understand why? I don't
think you do. Painting is a short cut to the subconscious,
Joan. Doctors don't have time to study rewrites of *Anna
Karenina;* six hundred pages to find out the patient wants
to throw herself under a train. Why won't you co-operate?

JOAN: There's more than one way.

> **ERIC** *moves away again.*

Signor Dottore Marcello... My Italian Doctor friend,
distinguished....

ERIC: Joan, there's doctors everywhere. All you need for a
doctorate is a dictionary and a pair of bifocals. You're too
easily impressed. Stop all this... Before it's too late.

Pause.

JOAN: (*trying to remember*) Signor Dottore Marcello... His
recommendation: Write a poem. "Poetry sharpens
perception. Crystallise your memory. One day someone
may discover your words. Preserve this moment in time".
You've never said anything like that.

ERIC: I'm not an ageing gigolo with one grubby white suit.
(*beat*) Oh, and before you accuse me of spying on you,
everyone strolls through the Piazza San Marco every day.

JOAN: He's in his forties. That's not old.

ERIC: It is for a gigolo. At forty, Italian gigolos are pensioned off.

JOAN: You saw him. When?

Silence, she looks at ERIC *for some response.*

You *were* following me.

ERIC: You're my wife.

JOAN: I feel differently now. Venice set me thinking. The City of Dreams. Everyone goes to Venice, sooner or later. Everyone strolls through the Piazza San Marco. You said it looks like a giant jig-saw puzzle.

ERIC: We've got the jig-saw puzzle. That's what gave me the idea. Don't you remember? One thousand pieces, The Piazza San Marco by Canaletto. I thought it would occupy your mind. I thought you'd like it.

JOAN: I do. If you love art, you love Venice. And now I've been there. Thank you for taking me. (*beat*) Thank yoooo! OK?

ERIC: Not to talk to strange men. (*he looks at his watch*)

JOAN: (*sigh*) I said, thank you for taking me. When the doorbell goes, Eric, we'll know it's the taxi. Don't keep looking at your watch.

ERIC: This is the problem, Joan. I only have to glance at my watch...

JOAN: The first of many. We were about to open the wine, then… How come this is the worst half hour of our lives? What did I say?

ERIC: (*heavy sigh*) I'm very sorry I said you were stupid.

JOAN: Deeply stupid.

ERIC: But it's true, even if I was wrong to say so. I can't pretend any more. Spin fantasies around you? God knows, you've got enough of your own. I don't think a bottle of wine, as if you're still in the Piazza San Marco… (*pause*) I phoned my mother again. She thought I was Barry Manilow. At least she got the gender right. Strange how she always does. She can't think straight any more. You're lucky. You can when you want to, think straight. When you listen to proper advice, if you know what I mean, not this new-age outfit in Surrey.

JOAN: I *do* know what you mean. You want me back in a proper hospital, carry on taking the pills. I'm sorry, I've had enough of that. Tranquilisers numb my brain. Harmful chemicals, I'm not taking them any more.

ERIC: So be it. I'm talking about my mother…

JOAN: They hand out tranquilisers like sweets.

ERIC: She's 78 this week.

JOAN: I've thrown them down the loo, tranquilisers, beta-blockers, statins, the lot. A treat for the rats in the sewer.

ERIC: Chemical castration? What a good idea. (*sighs*) Then I pray for your deliverance from the Slough of Despond. (*beat*) I do pray for you Joan.

JOAN: Every Sunday. But that still leaves Monday to Saturday.

Pause.

Know that Signor Dottore Marcello di Eduardo is an expert on art, music and literature. He's not an ageing gigolo.

ERIC: Doctor of what?

JOAN: Epi… Epigenomic variations in plants. Unfortunately, he can only get a job as a gardener.

ERIC: You said art expert.

JOAN: Eric, poets, dancers, painters, writers and scientists, all go to Venice. And some of them write about it. He reads them all. Can't I write about Venice as well in my own small way? You don't have to be a genius to go there.

Pause. **ERIC** *sits at the table.*

(*writing*) Venice shimmers in the morning sunlight, sharing it's joy with rich and poor alike. (*purring*) Shimmers y-e-e-e-s.

Yes St. Mark's cathedral was… I like that other cathedral more though… the day we got lost, that huge cathedral…

ERIC: Basilica.

JOAN: I'm writing in English. OK, basilica. Of course. Basilica, Basilica, Basilica. Must remember that, Basilica. The Basilica of San Paulo e San Giovanni.

ERIC: Basilica Santi Giovanni e Paolo.

JOAN: Santi?

ERIC: Plural.

JOAN: Eric…

ERIC: St. Paul. "We live by faith, not by sight."

JOAN: Good for St. Paul, but he wasn't a saint at the time. Basilica Santi Giovanni e Paolo. Interior; lofty splendour. Exterior; a massive… monolithic brick block. Who'd ever guess it? Inside the famous Madonna and Child by Bellini. And the one in the other place… the other cath… Basilica.

ERIC: Santa Maria dei Frari?

JOAN: You deserve a doctorate if you can remember all these names.

ERIC: (*pedantic*) Basilica Santa Maria Gloriosa dei Frari. I'll never forget that day. Talk about embarrassing. (*looks at his watch*)

JOAN: I'm talking about the painting. I was *not* causing a disturbance. When you put a coin in the box the painting lights up. You go tut tut tut. That's what's embarrassing. You lead the chorus of tut-tuts and shushes. So what if people were praying? It's not my fault the noise. A tinny little box. Want to see the child Jesus? Drop a coin in. Clunk!

As for the opera, what's the point of going with you? Oh, the Yorkshire Miner's Choir, yes. Signor Dottore Marcello invited me to the opera. I couldn't say "no", could I? By the way, he doesn't wear bifocals.

ERIC: Who paid for the tickets?

JOAN: (*beat*) Be honest, you'd have slept all through it. Snoring.

(*making a note*) My first opera, *Il Trovatore*. I still don't know what it means.

ERIC: *The Troubadour*. Minstrel.

JOAN: I didn't dare ask. I let him think I knew.

ERIC: You had money to spend. That's what he knew.

JOAN: (*making a note*) *The Troubador?* Is that all? An awful lot going on for one troubador. Nice music, needs a better story. Signor Dottore Marcello knows every word of it by heart. Nearly every word of every Italian opera. There's even an opera called *Signor Dottore!*

ERIC: Joan, he was toying with you.

JOAN: Pardon?

ERIC: Amusing himself. What d'you think he's doing now? Thinking of *you*? He works the bars and the hotels, and the Piazza San Marco. An unlicensed tourist guide touting

for business. A soft-porn gigolo, all promise and no
action. At large in Venice in a crumpled suit, and a fancy
pocket handkerchief for show. You paid for those opera
tickets. I know how much money you spent. Tell the truth.

Pause. **JOAN** *turns her wine glass upside down.*

You lied about the price of the paperweight. I bet he's
sold it back by now.

Pause.

JOAN: *He* gave me that book. The history of Venice in
pictures. Paintings, and engravings, but I can't look
any more in case I see that picture again, a man being
tortured in a dungeon. That's what's upset me. The
torture chamber in the Palazzo Ducale. A man in an iron
cage roasting alive. How could they be so cruel?

ERIC: It's only a picture. A warning to traitors. I'll get my
coat.

JOAN: Wait!

ERIC: D'you want yours?

JOAN: No wait. Oh dear… Look I…

   ERIC *goes out to get his coat.*

   She moves the glass an inch or two.

Eric! *Eric or Little by Little*, that's you! *Eric or Little by Little*,
fuss fuss fuss! You're so like your mother. *Eric or Little by
Little* your favourite book. Poor little Eric can do no right

at school, or on his journey on the high seas until he finds
God. After a life of sin, he returns home and dies fully
repentant, surrounded by the sweetness, light and moral
purity of his family. I've now read it three times.

ERIC *enters. He puts his coat over a chair.*

It's a short cut to *your* subconscious. But you've repented
already, Eric, so there's only death to come.

ERIC: What?

JOAN: *Eric or Little by Little*. Your book. Moral purity is
enforced by more immorality. Barbaric punishments and
executions.

JOAN *moves her wine glass about 2 inches along the table.*

ERIC: Did he tell you that? Joan, I'm trying to explain. While
I was talking to my mother, I realised…

JOAN *moves the empty wine glass another 2 inches along the
table.*

What are you doing?

JOAN: (*whispering loudly*) This world, Eric. This horrible,
horrible world. Signor Dottore Marcello is right. We
need more space ships. We've got to find true civilisation
wherever it is, but it's certainly not down here. It's out
there. It's out there somewhere.

ERIC: Where's this picture? Where's this damn picture! Joan,
it's only a picture in a book.

JOAN: The Bible's a book.

ERIC: If I ever meet this man…

JOAN: A man clapped in irons. They're stoking a fire under his feet. Another poor soul hangs from the ceiling, iron weights attached to him to increase his suffering beyond endurance, until his body splits apart and his entrails splatter on the ground. Venice, City of Dreams and horrific nightmares.

ERIC: Joan! These things happen everywhere. Why pick on Venice?

JOAN: But this time an artist has actually drawn it!

ERIC: And d'you know what? He was told to. He has no choice, or he did from a description, interviewing the torturers' apprentice.

ERIC sits down at the table sighs.

This picture has blown up in your mind out of all proportion. D'you understand? *(pause)* I'll try again. Look, Joan. It's wrong but it's life. On this planet, anywhere, or beyond our solar system, anything that lives and breathes suffers pain. It's a biological fact of life. We are made of flesh and blood. Even the son of God shared our physical suffering. "Father, forgive them for they know not what they do". Don't the last words of our Lord Jesus mean anything to you? No, they obviously don't.

He picks up his newspaper.

JOAN: I'm not painting any more.

ERIC: So paint *nice* pictures. Don't give up.

JOAN: After the splendours of Venice, a bowl of Tesco's fruit doesn't quite cut it. Words come easier to me now.

ERIC: This Signor Dottore character… Did you happen get his real name and address?

JOAN: Why?

ERIC: We should tip off the police in case he plies his trade here.

JOAN: Our meeting in Venice was perfect. Like a flower that blooms for a day.

ERIC: (*beat*) He's brainwashed you… Joan, he's a crank. You're getting the best available treatment here. You don't need this… You don't need pseudo… Pseudo whatever! Get over it. Jesus did and he was in agony on the cross. *You've* got a nice flat with central heating.

JOAN: Rented.

Pause.

ERIC: (*hurt*) Thank you, Joan. Thank you for reminding me.

He puts his paper down, gets up and stares out of the window.

JOAN: Redundancy, for going on about Jesus at work!

ERIC: Don't worry. I know what to do.

JOAN: I can't go back to that hospital. The group therapy
  leader fancies me. Tight Jeans, he doesn't even try to hide
  it.

ERIC: Joan, really!

JOAN: He stands too close when he looks at my paintings.
  One hand on my shoulder, the other hand twitching in his
  pocket. You know what I mean. Women do notice these
  things.

ERIC: Joan, this is not normal.

JOAN: It is to me. It's happening to me.

ERIC: So you're off to Surrey to join the yoga loving,
  vegan, chanting, meditating, chick-pea crackpots? Does
  that make any sense? If this is what you call a normal
  conversation…

JOAN: We still share the same bed but we can't have a normal
  conversation.

ERIC: We share the same bed because we haven't got another
  one.

  A terrible pause. Neither knows what to say next. Eventually…

JOAN: I often lie awake and listen to your heart beating.
  In the dark you look like a whale. Sometimes I wonder
  "how many more heartbeats will there be?" And why?
  Then one night you spoke. You said "We're going to
  Venice". I thought "The Kraken Wakes". What does it say?
  (*ponderous*) "We're going to Venice." Not "Would you like
  to go to Venice?"

ERIC: I borrowed money from my mother.

JOAN: You don't have to tell me.

ERIC: Barely enough to feed us and you're buying expensive opera tickets and wine for strangers at clip-joint prices. More rubbish to carry back here.

JOAN: One bottle of wine without your say so, your blessed authority. Chianti Classico. It's only Chianti Classico.

ERIC: I have to pay it back.

JOAN: No, you don't.

ERIC: I ought to. She runs that flat on a pension. Scrimps and saves just to buy me cakes for tea.

JOAN: Cakes. Remember that American couple? Fat woman with a thin husband. Always in the lobby. They live on cakes. I said "Where's a good place to eat?" "Oh, we don't eat," they said. "We graze." Like Tweedledum and Tweedledee they trundle off to buy more cakes. Maybe I'll write a poem entitled *The Cake Shops of Venice*. Or, *Cakes and Donkey Stew*. If you wander off the beaten track you *can* find donkey stew. Signor Dottore knows where to find it. Off the beaten track Eric. No maps, explore.

You and your careful budget. Every day the menu touristico. Escalope and spaghetti. Not once did we have seafood risotto either. Venice is famous for it. Seafood risotto.

ERIC: Risotto alla Pescatora. (*reverie*) Yes, I remember.

JOAN: You took me to Venice, yet you *didn't* take me to Venice. It was Signor Dottore Marcello di Eduardo who opened my eyes. *Art* brainwashes you. That's what he says. *Art* feeds us myths and lies. *Art* idealises nature, yet nature never needs it. *Art* shows us an idealised world which doesn't exist. Only when art reveals man's inhumanity to man does it tell the truth in those pictures of torture and brutal executions. I remember his words because he made me write them down. Don't allow art to fool you. Write the truth, only the truth, let your mind do the work and don't watch television. Another drug we're all addicted to. (*beat, taking up her pen*) Blood and Gold.

Pause. She moves the glass nearer to the edge of the table.

ERIC: (*dreamy*) Risotto alla Pescatora. (*he smiles to himself*)

JOAN: What?

ERIC: Er… What you said. Risotto alla Pescatora.

JOAN: So why not try it, once at least?

ERIC: I did.

JOAN: No you didn't.

ERIC: When you went off on your own. (*he looks at his watch*) You were gone for ages. What did you expect me to do?

She moves the empty wine glass again. **ERIC** *observes this warily.*

JOAN: Does this sulking going go on all day? You're not right in the head, but it's me who's sent to the loony bin. Take a look at yourself. I know you had a difficult childhood but you've had half a century to get over it.

Listen: church. I can't go to church with you anymore.

You aspire to mediocrity. That's what Signor Dottore Marcello says. You aspire to mediocrity. He took my hand and said so.

ERIC: He doesn't even know me. (*beat*) He took your hand?

JOAN: Oh, don't start!

Pause. She moves the wine glass an inch or two.

ERIC: Taking you to Italy was obviously a mistake. My mother was right. A waste of time and money. She was right.

Starts to make notes. She breaks off momentarily to move the glass again towards the edge of the table.

JOAN: I did enjoy it in my own way. Five nights in Venice, two nights in Rome. Marcello asked me what I thought...

ERIC: Marcello now.

JOAN: ...what I thought of the Sistine Chapel. He says it's not God on the ceiling, the creation of Adam and all that. Michelangelo knew a lot of muscle men.

ERIC: Joan, if ever you needed hospitalisation...

JOAN: (*aloof*) The title of my poem! *Blood and Gold*. The first line... Venice shimmers.... Shimmers... Well, I can't say sparkles, sounds like Oxford Street.

She stares dangerously at the wine glass.

ERIC: I hope you keep your appointment.

JOAN: I haven't got one.

ERIC: Did you cancel it? Joan! (*pause*) I see. A top consultant
psychiatrist accepts you as a patient on the NHS...

JOAN: He gives me nightmares. I told him. He climbed
through my bedroom window with a gun in his hand to
shoot me. So he says, "That's because you're afraid I'm
going to seduce you." On the National Health? Things are
looking up,

ERIC *moves the suitcase nearer to the door.*

But he *does* say I'm very perceptive. I've got a cap-and-
gown brain. It's true, I nearly went to university. So why
did you say I'm a deeply stupid woman? Why? *Why* do you
always tell people I'm an *amateur* painter? Why do you
say I write silly soft porn romances for bored housewives?
You watch me. Just you watch me. Eric or little by Little.
Mister stick-in-the-mud redundant English teacher.

Pause.

Answer me. Eric, you're the Church Warden. You haven't
taken a vow of silence. At least not yet.

Pause.

ERIC: I've got a job. Start next week. Remember Dickie
Pearson? Richard and Winnie? I bumped into them. He's
the manager of a nice hotel not far from mum.

JOAN: Bumped into them where?

ERIC: Venice.

JOAN: Venice?!

ERIC: The night before we left. You were at the opera. *(pause)* I'll be staying at mum's to cut the journey time.

JOAN: A job? Now you tell me.

ERIC: Only a concierge, but it's a job. Know that I mean it, Joan. Venice has affected us both.

He looks at her, and resolutely says no more. He waits by the window looking for the taxi.

You see…

JOAN: Because I went to the opera? What do you mean you've got a job? Just like that you've got a job and you're staying at your mother's place? Casually drops it into the conversation. *(forcing back tears, she makes notes)* So I went to the opera. Marcello took me. I didn't ask to go. *He* took me to the opera, the Teatro del Fenice.

ERIC: Teatro la Fenice.

JOAN: The only night we could get tickets.

ERIC: *You* bought the tickets. That night I planned to take you to a good restaurant. They do a Risotto alla Pescatora. But you spent too much on those opera tickets. You took a dried up old gigolo to the opera! I need money.

He paces about.

JOAN: *You* need the money! *(pause)* You knew all this time. You knew from the moment we left Venice. You knew!

Pause.

(writing) Signor Dottore Marcello wore a white linen suit and a straw hat.

ERIC: Ah, the love story. The would-be Helena Bonham Carter.

She moves the wine glass.

JOAN: *(writing, drifting into her thoughts)* "My nice English lady, you have a deep desire to be free. So be free." "But what if you miss someone?" "Do you really miss this someone. Or the security?" "Well", I said. "I might miss them because I love them."

ERIC *looks at her. An emotional moment between them, the last one.*

Venice. Y-e-e-es. How lovely, but if there was no one there... no people. Would it still be lovely? Or just a lot of old stones.

Blood and Gold, Venice shimmers in the morning sunlight... You see Eric, you weren't there the moment my life changed.

ERIC: But Signor Dottore Marcello was.

ERIC *turns slowly and looks at her, such pain in his eyes.*

He was there.

JOAN: (*reading from her notes*) Evening in the Piazza San Marco. The ferries take the day-trippers away. I stroll towards my favourite café. I took my notebook. You can't just sit there, a woman alone. So I made notes. You know what Italian men are. They think every woman wants sweeping off her feet, so when I heard his voice. I didn't know it, but he'd been reading over my shoulder. What I'd written...

Tiny orchestras take turns to play. Tiny or tinny? Café orchestras take turns to play. The Byzantine backdrop, "Il Duomo San Marco". An now a mist, a veil drifting in from the canal, past St. Mark's and into the square. More music: a raucous little band with a drunken drummer, scattering the pigeons. Dancers follow the band. It's a wedding procession. The groom carries his bride across the square. They sing, they laugh. Where are they going? The happiest happiness you've ever seen. But only for a few minutes. (*beat*) They've gone now. Disappearing down a narrow lane. The music fades into the mist. The pigeons return. The tiny orchestras strike up a tune. Strauss of all things. And why, I thought, did all of St. Mark's Square take so little notice? Because, in Venice, on holiday, in the Piazza San Marco, happiness happens all the time.

ERIC: And they don't skin people alive. Civilisation *has* moved on.

She moves the wine glass.

ERIC *looks at her and then sits down.*

JOAN: While I'm away I'll finish my poem. You never know, I might find a publisher. The psychiatrist? He'll only say it's a casebook study of a frustrated artist who sees Venice and... feels her art dying inside her. Signor Dottore Marcello is trying to save me. Don't you understand? I must be in control of my own life.

Open the wine Mr. Stick-in-the-mud. Celebrate your new job. Celebrate going home to mummy.

She moves the wine glass.

I see. I'm untalkable to again? Am I still untalkable to? Untalkable to by Mr. High and Mighty, or what? Mr. High-and-Judge-and-Condemn-Mighty? I'll say! What? Mr. Punish-and-Never-Forgive-High-and-Majestic-Mighty budget boss! Where is this bloody hotel!

ERIC: My taxi's due in ten minutes.

JOAN: *Your* taxi!

She fingers the glass dangerously.

ERIC: Yes.

JOAN: What about *my* taxi?

ERIC: I booked two taxis Joan. You can make your own way to Cranksville.

JOAN: So! Only ten minutes to go with Mrs. untalkable to? Are you sure? How many breaths will we draw in that time? How many heartbeats to go? How many heartbeats together? How many heartbeats for the rest of our lives? How many ticks in a clock?

ERIC: Joan, it took the miracle of the universe to put you on this planet. Is this rambling the best you can do?

JOAN: Me. Mrs nice English Lady Untalkable To.

ERIC: Joan! That's enough! Enough! I'm not in the mood.

JOAN: Oh, you're not in the mood? *You're* not in the mood? Mr. Too-Superior-to-Talk-to-his-Wife?

ERIC: What do we share? Nothing. Together we live apart.

She moves the glass another inch towards the edge of the table.

JOAN: Mr. Censorioso-Supremo. Huh! He now deserts his sick wife.

ERIC: So you *do* know you're…sick.

She bites her tongue and edges the glass another inch towards the edge of the table.

JOAN: Where's the wine in this glass? Happy wine. Red for cheerfulness wine.

Pause.

I do share things with you. I watched the cricket with you, didn't I? If I can watch a bore-a-saint-stiff cricket match… Cricket's not bad if you've got a good book.

You might at least look at me. No? So you're deserting me. Off to a nameless hotel in a nameless town. What a schemer you are. My father was right about you. Never trust a man who doesn't look at you as he's talking to you.

She pushes the glass a little closer to the edge of the table.

Staying with your mother? How long for?

ERIC *glances at his watch.*

The name of the hotel please. Whatsisname, Dickie
Pearson. Richard Pearson, hotel manager. I'll find him.
(*rummages through her handbag*) Where's my mobile? Did
you pack my charger? My Dad always said, "Joan, the
inside of your handbag is like the inside of your mind".
He said you were a stick-in-the-mud.

*Pauses, handbag open. She nudges the glass near to the edge
of the table. She rummages through her handbag. Some of the
contents fall out.*

People don't know. They don't know what I live with every
day.

*She picks up the contents of her handbag and piles them on the
table.*

I'm not a Schizo. I'm a bit upset, that's all. Why say things
like that? Schizo! You're right. He's a top psychiatrist. I
ought to be more grateful. If the Queen went mad, they'd
call my psychiatrist. Hah!

*She stuffs her possessions back into her handbag, but in the
middle of it she stops to push the wine glass a little nearer to the
edge of the table.*

ERIC *snatches the bottle of wine and puts it to one side.*

ERIC: If I stay, I'll call an ambulance to take you to your psychiatrist. *(posh)* By appointment to the Queen.

JOAN: You know what I mean! I didn't mean the Queen! You know I didn't mean the Queen. Don't look at me, accusing me as if I did mean the Queen. Oh God, for the rest of our lives you'll always believe it, believe I meant the Queen.

I didn't mean the Queen!

ERIC *looks at his watch.*

She moves the wine glass again.

Marcello di Eduardo told me where to go. So I rang them. I know what I'm doing. I don't need psychiatry. I must be… reborn. *We can* be reborn. You know where to find me.

ERIC: Over the bloody rainbow? I looked them up. They're organic vegans. A Spiritual Spa they call it. The only treatment allowed is meditation. They believe their founder came to earth in a flying saucer in 1985. His picture is on their website. I swear he's Chinese. I don't suppose it matters whether he fetched up on the South Downs in a flying saucer or a four by four.

JOAN: What matters is the teaching. It's a new way to live.

ERIC: Shut up.

ERIC *leaves the room.* **JOAN** *pushes the glass right to the edge of the table.*

JOAN: I'm only going for a fortnight. Marcello and I, we never… It really wasn't like that, Eric. He showed me the way. A new way.

ERIC *returns. He has his own bag and a raincoat.*

I'm sorry I called you names. Oh, what happened in Venice?

ERIC: Venice? What happened? I'll tell you. (*pause*) A long time ago when I first tasted Risotto alla Pescatora… I can't forget it. Most of all I can't forget the angel on the other side of the table. Her face haunts me every day of my life. In my mind's eye, still there when I die. Far better *you* won't be there. Barbara. (*pause*) She came from a good family. Me, the son of a van driver. One of her father's van drivers. We eloped in a way. Left a note for our parents and took the train all the way to Venice by ourselves.

Risotto alla Pescatora. The last night which I wrote in my diary. After dinner we strolled along the Riva Schliavoni, back to our hotel. The Grand Canal, the dappled moonlight in the water, like a Canaletto painting at night. Our last night in the hotel was…platonic. I was too much in love to… So we held hands and hardly spoke. I couldn't sleep either. On the journey home we were like strangers. When we arrived we parted too quickly. I said "When will I see you again?" A tiny frown, a flicker of a smile, and she was gone. A slim white coat and a pink travel bag getting smaller and smaller in the distance, and then she was swallowed by the crowd.

JOAN *tips the glass onto the floor and it shatters.*

ERIC *looks at the broken glass in horror.*

The doorbell rings.

JOAN: Eric! Send him away! I'm not going! Ok, I won't go!

ERIC: It's for me.

ERIC *goes out. The front door slams.*

JOAN: Oh! Eric, wait! Oh, why? Why, Eric, why?

(*silently*) Why? Why? Why? Why……

*As she mouths the word "why", fade in Tchaikovsky's October on piano. The light fades and lingers, ghostly, on **JOAN**'s face for a while.*

THE END